Seagulls
Soar

April Pulley Sayre

Illustrated by
Kasia Bogdańska

BOYDS MILLS PRESS
AN IMPRINT OF BOYDS MILLS & KANE
New York

Seagulls swerve.
Seagulls soar.
Yack! Yack! Yack!
from ship to shore.

Seagulls paddle,
seagulls float.
They skim a wake.
They board a boat!

Great Salt Lake
to desert dry,
far from sea,
gulls surf the sky.

Seagulls circle.
Truckloads tip.
Gulls on garbage
rip and flip.

Seagulls follow.
Tractors plow.
Insects turned up?
Seagulls chow!

Seagulls hunt,
stalk, and stare.
Seagulls dance,
pose, and pair.

Fishing buddies
clean their catch.
Seagulls squabble.
Seagulls snatch!

Seagulls carry.
Drop. *Smack! Smack!*
Shells hit pavement.
Clamshells crack.

Whale mouths push.
Trapped fish leap.
Seagulls catch.
Seagulls keep!

Seagulls nest,
gather sticks.
Spotted eggs, then . . .

. . . spotted chicks!

Seagulls preen.
Seagulls sun.
Left wing, left leg,
stretch as one.

Seagulls grow.
Seagulls hop.
From a cliff edge,
seagulls drop.

Seagulls swerve.
Seagulls soar.
Yack! Yack! Yack!
from ship to shore.

Seagulls: The Learning Birds

Some birds have only one way of finding a meal. Not seagulls! Seagulls are omnivores, meaning they eat many different kinds of food. On rocky shores, gulls hunt tide pools for snails, clams, fish, and shrimp. On sandy beaches, gulls eat mole crabs, horseshoe crab eggs, and jellyfish. In meadows, gulls dine on grasshoppers, flies, sunflower seeds, stink bugs, bird eggs, mice, moles, and even blueberries! This is just a sampling of the gull menu.

Seagulls are clever. They observe other animals, including humans. Gulls local to one area can invent a foraging (food gathering) trick not common elsewhere. Here are a few of the ways gulls gather food:

- In shallow water, Ring-billed Gulls paddle their feet to stir up sand to find small crustaceans and marine worms. Then they eat them.
- Ring-billed Gulls swoop down to grab insects in midair. California Gulls run, open-mouthed, through the thick clouds of tiny flies that hatch from salt lakes. They snap their bills closed, then open them again to eat more flies.
- Ring-billed Gulls, Herring Gulls, and Laughing Gulls gather at landfills and pick through trash for food. On beaches, they pull food out of trash cans or bait buckets.
- Mew Gulls flutter among plants, picking and eating moth caterpillars.
- During plowing and harvesting, Franklin's Gulls follow tractors. The tractors turn up hidden grubs or scare up flying insects the gulls can eat. Gulls may help farmers by getting rid of plant-eating pests. But when other foods are scarce, gulls may eat crops, too.
- A statue of gulls in Salt Lake City's Temple Square memorializes the gulls that, according to legend, gobbled a plague of katydids eating farmers' crops in June of 1848. The California Gull is the state bird of Utah and is common near Utah's Great Salt Lake.
- Heermann's Gulls plunge into water to grab sardines. They may also snatch food from a sea lion or sea otter.
- Gulls follow shrimp boats. The crew pulls up nets that contain fish and many other sea creatures. But the crew only picks out the shrimp. Gulls feast on the bycatch— the dead or dying fish dumped back into the ocean. Gulls also follow other kinds of boats because the boat propellers mix the water, pushing fish to the surface.
- Herring Gulls and Mew Gulls pull clams out of the water, then fly up above roads and drop the clams onto pavement to crack them open.
- Gulls fly or paddle close to humpback whales that are feeding. As the whales surface, gulls catch fish that are trying to flee from the whales. Sometimes gulls swoop to grab fish right out of a whale's mouth!

The Strange Case of the Worm Charmers and the Seagull Dance

Herring Gulls stamp on dirt, doing a quick step a little like an Irish step dance. In response, earthworms crawl out of the ground. The gulls eat the worms.

People once assumed that the earthworms came to the surface because the vibration made by the dancing gulls was similar to the sound of falling rain. (After rain, worms often crawl out onto the surface to escape flooded tunnels.) But neuroscientist Dr. Ken Catania of Vanderbilt University found that it's more likely that the vibration is similar to the digging sounds of moles, which hunt earthworms. The earthworms may be surfacing in an attempt to flee from moles tunneling in the dirt beneath them.

Gulls, by the way, aren't the only ones who use vibrations for hunting worms. In Appalachia, some people use a similar trick, called "worm charming," to gather earthworms for fishing bait. Worm charmers rub pieces of iron against wood stakes sunk in the ground. This makes the wood stakes vibrate, which brings earthworms to the surface.

Seagull Detectives

Identifying gulls is a tricky, enjoyable challenge for birdwatchers. Here's why:

- Gulls' feather patterns vary by season and age. Their bills, legs, and eyes change colors from season to season, as well.
- Immature gulls tend to have more brown feathers. (The adults have white, blue-gray, and black feathers, depending on species.)
- Large gulls may take four years to mature to adulthood. Along the way, their feather patterns shift. So, an experienced birdwatcher may be able to identify a bird not just as a "Great Black-backed Gull" but as a "first winter Great Black-backed Gull," instead.
- Adult feather patterns shift, too. For instance, adult Laughing Gulls have dark heads during breeding season, when they're courting. Then they molt—gradually dropping those dark feathers and growing pale, white-and-gray winter feathers for non-breeding season.

Seagull, Shore Gull, or Just Gull?

Seagull is a common name used for many species of birds in the family Laridae. But seagulls don't spend a lot of time far out at sea as albatrosses and other seabirds do. Many seagulls might better be called shore gulls. Most do live near water, but that water may be a lake or river. Seagulls nest in large groups called colonies, often on cliffsides and islands, but a rooftop in a city will do.

Gray Gulls nest in Chile's Atacama desert, with some nesting more than a hundred miles from the sea. The parents commute, flying to sea to catch fish, then back to the desert to feed nestlings. It's no wonder some birdwatchers shy away from the word *seagull*, using just *gull* instead.

Both *gull* and *seagull* are common names. Common names often differ from language to language and place to place. That can cause confusion. So, scientists agree on standard scientific names for each species. *Leucophaeus atricilla*, for example, is the scientific name for the Laughing Gull. (Laughing gulls, by the way, get their common name from their laugh-like call.) Scientists from all countries can use a scientific name and know they are talking about the same type of creature.

Whatever you call these birds, they are certainly worthy of study. They are acrobatic fliers. They are clever. They are flexible enough to adapt to changing conditions and umpteen habitats. Seagulls are survivors.